POLICE CRIME PREVENTION

Rescue and Prevention: Defending Our Nation

POLICE CRIME PREVENTION

MICHAEL KERRIGAN

MASON CREST PUBLISHERS
www.masoncrest.com

Mason Crest Publishers Inc.
370 Reed Road
Broomall, PA 19008
(866) MCP-BOOK (toll free)
www.masoncrest.com

First printing

1 2 3 4 5 6 7 8 9 10

Library of Congress Cataloging-in-Publication Data on file
at the Library of Congress

ISBN 1-59084-406-8

Editorial and design by
Amber Books Ltd.
Bradley's Close
74–77 White Lion Street
London N1 9PF
www.amberbooks.co.uk

Project Editor: Michael Spilling
Design: Graham Curd
Picture Research: Natasha Jones

Printed and bound in Jordan

Picture credits
Federal Emergency Management Agency: 6; Topham Picturepoint: 8, 11, 12, 15, 16, 17, 18,
20, 23, 24, 26, 27, 28, 30, 33, 34–35, 36, 38–39, 40, 43, 44, 47, 48, 51, 52, 53, 54, 55, 56,
57, 58, 60, 62, 63, 64, 67, 68, 69, 71, 72, 74, 76, 77, 79, 80, 82, 83, 85, 87, 88–89.
Front cover: Topham Picturepoint, Popperfoto (center).

DEDICATION

This book is dedicated to those who perished in the terrorist attacks of
September 11, 2001, and to all the committed individuals who continually
serve to defend freedom and protect the American people.

CONTENTS

INTRODUCTION

September 11, 2001, saw terrorism cast its lethal shadow across the globe. The deaths inflicted at the Twin Towers, at the Pentagon, and in Pennsylvania were truly an attack on the world and civilization itself. However, even as the impact echoed around the world, the forces of decency were fighting back: Americans drew inspiration from a new breed of previously unsung, everyday heroes. Amid the smoking rubble, firefighters, police officers, search-and-rescue, and other "first responders" made history. The sacrifices made that day will never be forgotten.

Out of the horror and destruction, we have fought back on every front. When the terrorists struck, their target was not just the United States, but also the values that the American people share with others all over the world who cherish freedom. Country by country, region by region, state by state, we have strengthened our public-safety efforts to make it much more difficult for terrorists.

Others have come to the forefront: from the Coast Guard to the Border Patrol, a wide range of agencies work day and night for our protection. Before the terrorist attacks of September 11, 2001, launched them into the spotlight, the courage of these guardians went largely unrecognized, although in truth, the sense of service was always honor enough for them. We can never repay the debt we owe them, but by increasing our understanding of the work they do, the *Rescue and Prevention: Defending Our Nation* books will enable us to better appreciate our brave defenders.

Steven L. Labov—CISM, MSO, CERT 3
Chief of Department, United States Search and Rescue Task Force

Left: A reassuring presence on the streets of our cities, the police officer does much to discourage crime and apprehend offenders.

CRIME, THE DISEASE...

Crime blights American society—and, indeed, many societies around the world—eating away at the fabric of our nation. In the most prosperous country on earth, life is impoverished for many by anxiety and fear; in times of peace, crime has turned our inner cities into virtual war zones.

It is not just the horrors of large-scale **narcotrafficking** or mass-murder that make for misery. "Minor" crimes, such as vandalism, are also a major problem. How are we to tackle the problem? In recent years, police officers and **criminologists** have been considering this question in some depth, and have come up with new ideas and initiatives for catching criminals. More intriguing, however, they have also been reviewing the traditional role of a "reactive" police force—which responds to a call from the community after a crime has been committed. Now, experts are asking whether many crimes could not be prevented in the first place, and are developing techniques and programs designed to do just that. Society needs to be

Left: In our most disadvantaged inner-city communities, family life for many has broken down under the relentless pressure of poverty, drugs, and crime. Police officers, like these in New Jersey, often find themselves trying to take on the task of acting as advisors and role models.

able to punish criminals, but it is equally important that would-be criminals find it difficult to offend at all. For the disease of crime, prevention is better than cure.

A PROBLEM SOLVED?

We love movies or novels in which police or private detectives solve crimes, but the police—and the victims of crime—know that the reality is often less satisfactory. The arrest and conviction of the criminal may come as a relief, but it is not a "solution" to the pain and misery that has been caused. It will not bring back the murder victim to a devastated family, or restore the peace of mind to a senior citizen now too afraid to venture out; nor will it rebuild the confidence of the victim of rape or other assault.

"Property crimes" are often seen as of secondary importance to crimes against persons. It is true that most of us would sooner suffer the loss of a material item than be badly injured. Yet, while this theory is true on its surface, the distinction does not take into account the fact that "mere" possessions are invariably invested with strong personal emotions. For example, the husband and wife whose home has been burgled may feel an all-but-physical sense of violation as they survey the mess and damage the intruders have left behind. A few dollars' worth of jewelry may represent generations of tradition for the family in which they have been handed down.

The theft erases a link with the family's past, striking a blow against that family's sense of itself. An arrest and an insurance payment will not compensate such people for their loss. Nor will the successful conviction of the criminal amount to a solution of the

Relaxed, but ready for anything, officers of the Capitola Police Department, California, patrol the seafront. A balance always has to be struck between maintaining a police profile and setting people at their ease—in a beach resort, this can be particularly challenging.

"PRISONERS IN OUR OWN HOME"

"We used to be trusting; we weren't suspicious of anyone, but now we keep our doors locked all the time," said 83-year-old Blasco Scrofano to Fernanda Santos of the *New Hampshire Eagle-Tribune*. That was before Wayne J. Cameron, 34, forced his way into the Scrofanos' home in Lawrence, New Hampshire, and beat the elderly couple with an iron crowbar. A long-term heroin addict with a string of previous convictions, Cameron left Blasco and Beatrice Scrofano in no doubt that he meant business. He hit Mr. Scrofano twice as he knelt to open the safe in which he kept jewelry and savings.

Cameron made off with $10,000 in cash and valuables, but the damage he had done to his victims was far more than monetary. "This man left me in fear," said Mrs. Scrofano, "and this is a fear that will never leave me." Cameron was eventually caught and sentenced to serve two concurrent 20-year terms, but Blasco and Beatrice feel that they, too, are doing time—always on edge, afraid to go out. "We are prisoners in our own home," said Mr. Scrofano.

The fear of crime can be almost as damaging as the reality for those who live alone or are vulnerable: too many Americans are afraid to leave their homes.

crime. The real triumph would be for the offense not to have taken place to begin with, and this is the goal toward which crime prevention programs are directed.

COUNTING THE COST

A recent article in the *Journal of Law and Economics* by social scientist David Anderson assessed the cost of crime to the U.S. economy at a staggering $1.7 trillion a year. This figure, it must be emphasized, is achieved by comparing current costs of criminal activity with those of an imaginary paradise in which there was never any crime at all. In such a **utopia**, there would, for example, be no need for any money to be spent on safes—or even locks for doors and windows.

These security measures now cost Americans $4 billion a year. With no need for jails, we would save $35 billion; we could also do without our present $1.4-billion expenditure on surveillance cameras. The redundancy of computer virus checkers and associated security would release an additional $8 billion. Guard dogs alone cost Americans $49 million a year.

Altogether, crime costs us far more than we think—before we even consider the actual cash value of stolen property. Each year, our society spends $8.9 billion a year on medical treatment for the victims of crime—even those not directly affected feel financial pain by paying tax contributions to federal welfare programs and higher health insurance premiums. Total expenditure on what Anderson calls "crime-related production"—the provision of products or services made necessary by crime (such as window locks, safes, security alarms, special fencing, and security guards)—comes to more than $397 billion every year—more than $1,000 for every person in the United States.

Yet this is just the beginning. Consider, for example, what economists call the "opportunity costs" of crime—all the other things we could do with the time and money we currently commit to this problem. Again, Anderson bases his calculations assuming a crime-free utopia, in which no one ever had to lock a house or car. He estimates we spend four minutes every day seeing to the security of our property. Multiply this by the 365 days in every year and the 200 million adults with property in the United States, and you can see how the wasted time adds up to a major cost to the economy— $89.6 billion, says Anderson.

Moreover, if criminals were working for a living, rather than making everybody else's life a misery or serving time, they could be contributing around $40 billion every year to the legitimate economy. And what of their victims? We have already considered the expense of treating them, but what of the production lost through their time off work?

The sums Anderson has calculated are staggering, although they have to be kept in perspective. None of us seriously expects to be able to live in a world without any crime. Yet if such expenditures could never be abolished altogether, is it unrealistic to hope that they might be significantly reduced? Think of the schools, hospitals, and other services we might fund with the money saved. Or, looking at the figures another way: the savings amount to $4,118 for each American, per year.

A "PROPERTY CRIME"

Burglars broke the heart of a mother from Liverpool, England, when they broke into her home and stole a camcorder with precious videos of her disabled daughter. They also made off with around £200 ($300) in cash raised by kindly neighbors to buy presents for her daughter, Gemma, age 5—but it was the loss of the videos that her mother, Cathy Collins, regretted most bitterly. "Gemma has the mental age of a two-year-old and she can no longer talk," she told a reporter from the local newspaper, the *Anfield and Walton Star*. "The reason we bought the camcorder was so we could see Gemma as she was," she explained. "We had film from last Christmas and her fifth birthday party, which is of no use to anyone but the family. I'm heartbroken that anybody could do this to us, especially to Gemma."

A broken window, a devastated life: even an apparently "minor" crime can have a profoundly distressing impact on its victim.

Their work disparaged by those who do not see it as "real" policing, and resented by "respectable" citizens who ought to know better, traffic cops are among the unsung heroes of American community life. Countless accidents are prevented and lives saved by the intervention of the traffic police—whose presence on the streets also helps discourage potential criminals.

LIVING IN FEAR?

Each year since 1999, the National Crime Prevention Council (NCPC) has conducted a survey of prevailing attitudes to discover how Americans feel about crimes in their communities. Findings for 2000, the most recent figures available, suggest that we are "safer than some of us think...but not as safe as we deserve to be." A large-scale and in-depth study, it uncovered interesting—albeit contradictory—concerns.

Despite seven years' steady fall in crime rates, more of us are afraid to walk the streets of our neighborhoods. Adults worry more about the safety of their children—yet take less trouble to ensure that safety. More children are left home alone and for longer periods; parents are more concerned, but go out anyway. What about safety at school? More parents are concerned about school

Police officers from Poughkeepsie, New York, talk to a business-owner and resident as part of a concerted effort to keep in touch with life on the city's streets. In the days of foot patrols, such contact came naturally: now officers have to work consciously to attain a similar rapport at sidewalk level.

violence than ever before, but relatively few worry specifically about bullying. Yet the latest official statistics suggest that bullying is spiraling out of control. As many as 75 percent of school students have been victims of bullying, according to several recent studies. Have the statisticians—or America's parents—got it wrong?

Asked about official crime prevention programs, people's responses were again contradictory. The bad news, as far as an organization like the NCPC is concerned, is that fewer people are

The writing is on the wall for this depressed district of New York City: if graffiti is ugly in itself, the signal it sends out is even more unappealing. This, it plainly says, is an uncared-for neighborhood, where criminality is rife. Law-abiding people will not wish to stay.

participating—or even seem to know about—community-level crime prevention programs. The good news is that more are reporting "engagement with" their immediate neighbors, meaning that they know and talk to them. Every study to date has found that when neighbors look out for one another, the work of the criminals is that much harder and crime rates fall.

COMMUNITY COLLAPSE

Nationwide figures for crime may seem awesome, but fears for our own safety tend to be exaggerated. The chances of any one of us falling victim to a significant act of violence or other serious crime are, thankfully, slender. At the same time, however, while crime may not be as fearsome as we think, it may be more damaging than we realize. The sheer, daily nuisance-value of apparently "trivial" offenses takes quite a toll. Graffiti, burned-out cars, broken windows—such sights as these lend a dismal, depressing prospect to many inner cities. And, according to increasing numbers of experts, these images help create the sort of climate in which crime seems unexceptional, inevitable, and therefore acceptable—particularly to the young people living in these neighborhoods.

In this, experts are following the philosophy of George L. Kelling, a professor at Rutgers University, New Jersey, and Fellow of the Program for Criminal Justice Policy and Management of the John F. Kennedy School of Government, Harvard. From the early 1980s onward, Kelling proposed a policy known as **zero-tolerance** policing. Taken up enthusiastically by police forces in America and worldwide, its intention is not, as some critics have suggested, to

Police officers across America have been renewing their relationship with their public in recent years, in response to a feeling that an increasingly cruiser-bound force was becoming remote from the people it was supposed to be serving. Here, an officer stops to chat with a city storeowner, making time to listen to his concerns.

"criminalize" whole communities of largely innocent citizens, but to establish the authority of the police officer—and thus the law—on every street.

In some ways, this represents a return to old-fashioned policing values. But it is also a radical shift, turning policing priorities upside down. Kelling's criticism was that police officers were turning a blind eye to petty offenses at the street level because they felt they had more important crimes to deal with. There was neither the time nor the resources, they argued, to bother with matters like drinking in public or littering. Kelling argued that, on the contrary, law enforcement must begin with the basics. Look after these, he said, and the vast range of crime suddenly will seem more manageable.

In effect, this is a matter of simple pride. Where patrolling police officers take pride in the orderliness of a neighborhood, the people of that community are better able to maintain their own control. Where, by contrast, the little abuses are ignored, the whole neighborhood may be set for a downward slide. Kelling sketches a heart-sinking scenario, but one which is only too recognizable:

"A stable neighborhood of families who care for their homes, mind each other's children, and confidently frown on unwanted intruders can change, in a few years or even a few months, to an inhospitable and frightening jungle. A piece of property is abandoned, weeds grow up, a window is smashed. Adults stop scolding rowdy children; the children, in turn, become more rowdy. Families move out, single adults move in. Teenagers gather in front of the corner store. The merchant asks them to move; they refuse. Fights occur. Litter accumulates. People start drinking in front of the grocery; in time, a drunk slumps to the sidewalk and is allowed to sleep it off. Panhandlers approach pedestrians.

"At this point, it is not inevitable that serious crime will flourish or violent attacks on strangers will occur, but many residents think that crime, especially violent crime, is on the rise, and they modify their behavior accordingly. They use the streets less often and, when on the streets, stay apart from their fellows, moving with averted eyes, silent lips, and hurried steps. 'Don't get involved'."

THROUGH A BROKEN WINDOW

George Kelling is often credited with originating the **broken window theory**: the idea that if one broken window in a building is neglected, others will soon be broken, too. In fact, as he happily admits, the theory was already well established when Stanford psychologist Philip Zimbardo performed an interesting experiment in 1969. Two automobiles, without license plates, but in good condition, were left with their hoods up on streets in two districts—the Bronx, New York, and Palo Alto, California. In the Bronx, then a notorious inner-city district, the first vandals struck within 10 minutes. Over the next 24 hours, just about every salvageable spare part had been removed. Still, the destruction continued, as windows were smashed, seat covers slashed, and the interior turned into a children's playground.

In middle-class, law-abiding Palo Alto, the abandoned car survived intact for more than a week. Eventually, Zimbardo intervened, inflicting some damage himself to "start the ball rolling." And roll it certainly did! Within a few hours, this car, too, was a wreck.

What is particularly interesting about the experiment is that, in both cases, conventional assumptions proved incorrect. "Respectable" white adults inflicted most of the damage.

Kelling's work has had a profound effect on policing in recent years, but his conclusions have vast implications for citizens. Just as people need self-respect before others will respect them, so do wider communities. We all have a role to play in looking after the neighborhoods in which we live. If we do not care about litter or vandalism, why should outsiders? Crime prevention is not just about locking doors and windows, any more than crime is just about robbery, rape, or murder. Successful law enforcement starts with the individual citizen on the street.

A young boy looks into an abandoned apartment in downtown Dallas: crime thrives amid such dereliction and social decay. The young drug addicts who congregate here will commit crimes on the streets outside to fund their habits and the district's decline will continue.

BETTER THAN CURE...

Crime prevention makes no claim to be rocket science. On the contrary, it is founded in plain and practical common sense; and far from being a new idea, it is as old as crime itself. For as long as people have had possessions, they have taken trouble to keep them safe; for as long as there have been thieves, people have tried to exclude them.

While it is true that the officially coordinated crime prevention program is a relatively recent development, the underlying principles of such programs have been tried and tested over many centuries. The broken window theory is new as a sociological idea, but its essential insight into human nature is one that has been recognized from the earliest times.

The involvement of the police in crime prevention work is also not as innovative as it seems. Indeed, if anything, it represents a return to traditional policing values. Those who founded the first police forces never anticipated they would rush to respond to each emergency summons as it came. Rather, they saw officers patiently building security and social stability from the ground up.

Left: A Corpus Christi, Texas, police officer makes an arrest on the beach during spring break—early intervention can put a lid on a problem before it escalates out of hand. Such simple, down-to-earth thinking underlies all the most-effective police work; crime prevention is mainly a matter of common sense.

Police officers pound the beat down Boston's Homestead Street, or "Heroin Alley": once they would have breezed by in their cars, far removed from the realities of life down here. Successful community policing builds authority and order from the sidewalk up. There is no substitute for getting to know a neighborhood and its inhabitants.

FOUNDING PRINCIPLES

Humans are social animals by instinct, but that has never been a block to envy or aggression. Crime is one of the great eternals of the human condition. So, fortunately, is common sense. Crime prevention in its most primitive sense originated with the first person to hide a favorite flint blade where others would not find it. The streets of ancient Rome were as mean and murderous as those of any modern city; citizens understood that they had to take

SENSE ON THE STREET

Stay alert wherever you are—on the street, on public transportation, or in a mall.

● Get to know your neighborhood. If you sense something is wrong, know where you can get help—from police or a fire station, hospital, convenience store, restaurant, or public telephone.

● Avoid dark side streets at night. Also avoid shortcuts across vacant lots or parking lots at any time.

● Do not be obvious about money or jewelry. If you need to go to an automated teller machine, do it in the daytime; if you feel uneasy about people standing nearby, do not approach the machine at all.

● If you feel seriously uneasy about anything when you are out on the streets, shout good and loud!

This footbridge at a train station in London, England, offers an ideal ambush point for muggers.

precautions to protect themselves. The essentials of common sense have never changed. Then, as now, people lock their doors and windows, avoid dark streets and alleys, and do not advertise the fact that they are carrying valuables.

Neither have the founding principles of good policing changed, as established in the first half of the 19th century. Sir Robert Peel, the British statesman who inaugurated the world's first police force, took great pains to emphasize that these men were representatives of the communities they patrolled. Though they wore uniforms for ready recognition, he was anxious that they should not seem set apart from the people among whom they moved. "The police are the public," he insisted, "and the public are the police."

Like their English models, the first U.S. police officers in the 1840s walked routes, or "beats," which they came to know extremely well—if, that is, they did not already know them. They were naturally close to their communities, able to recognize the faces and know about local gossip—and as a result, their communities felt close to them.

Through much of the 20th century, however, police forces became increasingly professional and increasingly remote from a public whose sense of involvement in law and order was fast diminishing. It was an age of specialization, and police certainly needed

Left: "The police are the public, and the public are the police." The first police force in the modern sense was that established in 19th-century Britain by Sir Robert Peel, after whom they were affectionately known as "Peelers" or "Bobbies" by the British public.

The perception that the police are there as protectors of white privilege has done incalculable damage to America down the years— only recently, have serious steps been taken to correct it. Today, however, forces work hard to recruit able African-American officers and to address the concerns of African-American citizens.

the new skills and experience they were acquiring, for they now had to deal with organized crime and other large-scale problems. But the public was specializing, too, with people getting increasingly wrapped up in their jobs and cut off from their communities. A new breed of suburban commuters emerged who spent hardly any time in their "home" neighborhoods and who scarcely knew their neighbors. Most Americans were content to just bide by the law, with no sense that any more active engagement with the wider community

FACE TO FACE

In Wagga Wagga, a small city in New South Wales, Australia, police were concerned about the numbers of young men drifting by degrees into ever-more serious crime. At the same time, they believed victims felt that their sufferings were not recognized. Both were problems that needed to be addressed.

In an imaginative program, police officers arranged meetings between offending youths and their victims, to help young criminals appreciate that their actions had consequences, which often caused other people pain. The victims, for their part, felt that for the first time their experiences were recognized.

In days gone by, police officers were "community cops" who knew all the young people on their beats and who could offer informal advice and warnings from an early stage. They also knew the victims of crime, who appreciated their concern. Today, it takes an official program to recapture something of that old closeness, but it has certainly proved effective—with scores of satisfied victims and a 74 percent drop in youth crime.

might be required. Concerned citizens knew to call the police when a crime took place, but that was the limit of their responsibilities.

As both police and public were becoming ever more removed from their home communities, it was only criminals who were remaining loyal to their home turf. Day in and day out, most crime was still taking place on a small scale at a local level—and neither the police nor the public were well placed to respond.

NEIGHBORHOOD WATCH

As the 20th century evolved, the distance between police departments and the communities they served grew—and after World War II, it did so at an even greater rate. Cruising in cars and communicating with radios, officers were able to respond to any call at a moment's notice—but what they were unable to do was the patient meeting-and-greeting that builds relationships with their local community. Women joined the workforce—and joined their husbands on the morning train to the city—meaning that more homes were left unattended.

The crime prevention programs that sprang up toward the end of the 20th century were attempts to rebuild the bond between public and police that had been broken. As early as 1972, police chiefs and sheriffs understood the importance of good neighborly practice in discouraging crime. Stark differences in crime rates were reported between districts where people did report suspicions to law enforcement officers and districts where they did not. And this was not just about a readiness to call the police, experts surmised— surely that single statistic also represented a whole set of associated attitudes and local conditions.

In short, there was one sort of community where neighbors looked out for each other, and there was a second in which they told themselves, "It's not my problem." Programs were introduced, and

Right: Criminals are conscious of the risks they run where a community works together in neighborly vigilance: the mere sight of a sign like this one in East Austin, Texas, may deter some offenders.

over the next few years, these would evolve into **Neighborhood Watch**. The effects were dramatic and almost immediate. Burglaries in areas where the program was introduced fell by up to 75 percent. Not surprisingly, the program was quickly broadened in scope.

Since then, Neighborhood Watch and similar programs have flourished, helped by promotional campaigns, like that of the

National Crime Prevention Council (NCPC) and Crime Prevention Coalition of America (**CPCA**). Local police forces spearhead these nationwide initiatives, aimed at recruiting ordinary people into the fight against crime.

These campaigns drive home the same message as Sir Robert Peel: that the police and the public are one and the same, or that, as today's slogan puts it, crime prevention is "everybody's business."

In Boston, 12-year-old Tracina Tucker says goodbye to community police officer John Ridge, an old friend to residents of her Lenox Street housing project. But community policing is not all about meeting and greeting: here at Lenox Street police, they have cracked down aggressively on every sort of youth crime.

Police and public come together at a Syracuse, New York, community meeting: such encounters offer an opportunity for a two-way traffic in ideas and information. People who feel they have some stake in the policing of their community are far more likely to take a positive attitude toward their police.

This is often a difficult message to get to young people, who tend to resent any authority, particularly that of the police; their subculture may even encourage such suspicion. Yet many police officers are young themselves and share the enthusiasms of other young people. This recognition led the police department of Dayton, Ohio, to establish COP'RZ, while Middletown, Connecticut, has its Blue Crew. These rap and rock groups perform at young people's parties, bringing together two communities who have often been at odds.

Gradually, the bond between police and public is being renewed. The police are regaining some of the detailed understanding of local communities that their predecessors once had, and this in turn is cutting crime. A good example of this comes from Merseyside, England, where a "crime-mapping" program was established in

ON THE MOVE

During 1990, 840 million people made journeys by train in France, and 968 acts of violence on trains were committed. That ratio, in fact, makes rail travel in the country comparatively safe—but this was not the perception of the public in Paris. A major urban center, Paris has had all the usual big-city problems: travelers on its trains had to contend with everything from vandalism to vagrants. Again, actual violence was infrequent, but as George L. Kelling has pointed out, the perception of violence can be a profoundly damaging problem, since it creates the conditions in which violence is more liable to flourish.

Thus, those who could afford to do so—usually young, middle-class commuters—started finding other ways of traveling, and the rail network was left to the homeless and the criminal and to those who had no other means of transportation. The city's elderly felt especially vulnerable. The response of the authorities was twofold. First, they took active steps to improve safety on the system, with extra station staff, video surveillance, and panic alarms. They also supported social service programs aimed at integrating homeless people into Paris life and tackling juvenile delinquency.

1995. Assembling information on places where multiple offenses have taken place, police identified particular hot spots in areas already high in crime. Investment was then focused on those places in different forms—everything from the fitting of locks, lighting, and alarms to job training and sports programs for young offenders. Since the program began, emergency calls to the police have dropped by as much as 20 percent, cutting costs and cutting crime.

As the work of the police is seen to have an effect and the public regains its trust, the only losers are criminals. But this is a process without end, and it calls for imagination and goodwill, both now and in the future. The bond between police and public can be strengthened, but each side must be prepared to go out and meet the other halfway to rebuild our communities.

Cycle cops enter into the sunshine spirit of an afternoon in Venice Beach, California: their bikes give them mobility without setting them at a distance from those they serve.

A SAFER CITY

In discussing the work of crime prevention programs, there is little point concentrating on theory: these programs must work in practice, or they are no use at all. Although there are associated theories—the broken window theory, for example—these have been tested for so long and so rigorously that they now are considered common sense.

It is also important to remember that truly creative crime prevention thinking does not rely on just one theory. Rather, it approaches the problem from many different directions. Increased police presence, video surveillance, alarms, working with offenders, working with victims and would-be victims, repairs to street lamps, litter patrols, visits to daycare centers and schools: a typical crime prevention program can involve all these things and more. A number of different agencies, as well as the public, work together in the drive for a safer neighborhood and a higher quality of life.

This chapter focuses on one American city, looking at the ways its police and people tackled a crime problem that at one point seemed overwhelming. It has by no means been plain sailing all the way, nor could it be claimed that the war against crime has definitely been

Left: Officers of the New York Police Department are well equipped to deal with trouble at the city's St. Patrick's Day March, carrying bundles of plastic handcuffs to restrain the rowdy. Individual police forces know their public and the particular flashpoints of their year.

won, but the people of Fort Worth, Texas, feel strongly that their efforts have been worthwhile.

PREVENTION PIONEERS

Fort Worth, Texas, takes pride in being "the city where the West begins." It recently became home to the National Cowgirl Museum and Hall of Fame. A successful tourist industry has been built upon its fascinating history of the frontier days, and visitors come from all over the world to see the world's only daily cattle-drive in the city stockyards.

In addition to the rough romance of the old West, tourists are also drawn to Fort Worth by other attractions, particularly its world-famous Modern Art Museum, the biggest gallery of modern art outside New York. In truth, neither tourists nor Fort Worth's half-million population have felt any desire to experience Wild West-style lawlessness firsthand. By the 1990s, however, many citizens were finding their quality of life seriously affected by both the fear and the reality of crime.

PARTNERSHIP

Fort Worth was not alone in its problems. Other Texan cities were affected, which prompted the launch in 1992 of an initiative known as T-CAP. The Texas City Action Plan to Prevent Crime involved not only Fort Worth, but also Arlington, Austin, Corpus Christi, Dallas, Houston, and San Antonio. A partnership between seven cities, T-CAP encouraged and facilitated coordination and consultation between politicians, police departments, and public

The advent of closed-circuit television represents a revolution in crime prevention, although critics claim it simply displaces crime into unmonitored streets just outside the downtown centers.

With the help of her laptop computer, this police officer in Austin, Texas, can match cars to addresses, crimes to offenders, and property to victims in an instant. Computers have transformed modern police work, dramatically speeding the gathering and exchange of information on which successful policing depends.

service agencies across the state; more importantly, however, it also encouraged partnership within member communities.

All manner of agencies in Fort Worth have been involved in the program, from the police to educators, from housing authorities to health-care workers. Indeed, participation extends all the way down the city hierarchy to pest control, for no detail is too small (as is shown by the broken window theory). Local businesses are also involved, from major companies to corner stores: all have come together with ordinary citizens to discuss how their needs might best be served.

The involvement of as many individuals and interest groups as possible is, of course, important as a matter of democratic principle—but it serves another highly practical purpose, too. The more people feel that they are being consulted and that they have a voice in the running of their community, the more they will take pride in it and defend it. Is an act of vandalism just "one of those things"? Is a pile of litter to be dismissed as "someone else's problem"? Or are both to be resented as affronts to the community at large? How they are regarded depends on how much individual residents feel involved: is the neighborhood their home—or just some place where they have ended up living?

GRAFFITI WARS

It may seem a minor problem, but graffiti is unsightly and also depressing. Whatever the actual words, the meaning between the lines is clear: "We don't care how our neighborhood looks." That message, in turn, leads to acts of more serious vandalism and petty crime. Before you know it, a nice street is on the slide. But if graffiti is often the beginning of social disintegration for an entire neighborhood, it is also often an early step in a young offender's journey toward crime. There are two good reasons, then, for tackling graffiti as soon as it appears.

A PROBLEM PROJECT

In 1991, serious rioting broke out on the Meadow Well Estate, just outside the northern English city of Newcastle-upon-Tyne. It shocked everyone—except those living on the estate, who had been putting up with lawlessness for years. Yet the police had remained remote, and the community had collapsed, losing the will to defend itself.

The challenge was to rebuild that community. There had to be a greater, more personal police presence, and it had to come soon. The number, frequency, and intensity of uniformed patrols was increased. Persistent offenders were identified, cautioned, and, when necessary, detained; investigations were pursued, and prosecutions followed through with new determination. Meanwhile, officers took the time to get to know the law-abiding residents, listening to their information and advice, and also offering reassurance. This did much to foster better police-public relations on the estate. More importantly, it led to a dramatic drop in crime rates. Within three years, there was a 48 percent drop in the number of burglaries, a 27 percent reduction in the rate of criminal damage, and a 13 percent reduction in thefts from automobiles.

In Laval, Quebec, in Canada, police and courts have worked alongside city school boards, shops, and businesses in trying to clamp down on graffiti. Not only have young offenders been vigorously pursued and prosecuted, but they have also been required in many cases to repair the damage themselves. Shopkeepers and residents are encouraged to report offenses. One of the difficulties with what are

Race riots exploded in Burnley, northern England, in the summer of 2001, with gangs of white and Asian youths rampaging through the town, causing untold damage.

perceived to be "minor" crimes is that people start taking them for granted. In effect, the crime is accepted, taking the whole neighborhood another step down the slippery slope that can eventually lead to complete breakdown in law and order.

In a program in Haarlem in the Netherlands, a unique solution was found to this problem. The Schwarbroek Tunnel was, in theory,

Graffiti had been etched into this wall in Harlem, New York City, even before the cement that coated it was dry: damage and disfigurement were thus built into its very fabric. Our physical surroundings can be seen to set the tone for our lives at large: this street establishes a mood of dereliction and despair.

a right of way for pedestrians and cyclists, but few people ventured near, fearing it as a dark and dangerous haunt of violent youth gangs. In 1994, the local government took action, cleaning the tunnel completely and installing new lighting. The city's Linnaeus College then "adopted" the tunnel as a gallery for youth art, displaying the energy and creativity of Haarlem youngsters. Nor was this a one-time program. The Schwarbroek has a regularly changing calendar of events, just like any other art museum. General use of the tunnel has stayed high, which in turn has helped keep vandals at bay; there has been little new graffiti in the last few years.

SAFETY

In Fort Worth, T-CAP considered every aspect of safety in the city, not just security from criminal attack. Thus, the Fort Worth Police Department worked with the housing authority on a traffic plan to enhance road safety, while city government was pressed to provide better street lighting as a guard against both accidents and crime. This is an instance of a theory known as **CPTED** (pronounced "sep-ted")—Crime Prevention Through Environmental Design.

It sounds sophisticated, but CPTED has a core of common sense. The idea is that city planners, architects, and landscapers can program security into their designs from the very start, designing buildings and public spaces in which people will feel safe (and criminals will feel uncomfortable). Is that underpass well lit, or is it dark and threatening? Are the approaches open and inviting, or are there shadowy bushes or concrete angles where muggers may lurk? A path across an open area will feel a lot safer if a busy public basketball court has been placed nearby. When people feel safe and confident that the streets are their own and the more the public feels in control, the less that criminals feel they have scope for action. The purpose of CPTED is to make the reduction of criminal activity a basic objective of planning and design.

BEATING THE BULLIES

Studies in the 1980s revealed that 9 percent of schoolchildren in Norway were bullied. This was bad news, not only for them, but also for their country, as statistics also showed that those 7 percent of students who were picking on their classmates were four times more likely to become criminals as adults.

Rather than intervening aggressively, the Norwegian authorities decided on a large-scale campaign of education. An advice booklet was issued to teachers, and every parent with a school-age child was given a folder with information and advice about the problem. A video offering additional advice was available for anyone who asked, and the situation was monitored by means of questionnaires. Children were asked about their own experiences of bullying, if any, and the readiness of teachers and fellow students to help. Although there was no **punitive** campaign against the bullies, the issue was kept "live." At the end of two years, the number of bullying victims had fallen by 50 percent, and there were indications that vandalism, theft, and **truancy** had also fallen.

T-CAP also sponsored self-defense workshops to give citizens more confidence on the streets. Local laws and regulations were reviewed and rationalized in consultation between the police and the housing authority. One outcome was the banning of glass bottles, for reasons of general safety. It is a minor innovation, but when combined with many others, it can add up to a wholesale change in the quality of life.

Students in Syracuse, New York, meet their mentors from the city's police department regularly to build real relationships: here, Raphael Salami talks with "his" cop, Officer Mike Boni.

EDUCATION

Education is also a priority. In Forth Worth, this went beyond lecturing schoolchildren on the evils of crime. Local businesses were encouraged to provide scholarships and support for school activities. This promoted pride within the community, boosting not just the lucky students themselves, but also their families, neighbors, and classmates. And it gave students from disadvantaged backgrounds a reason to strive. It also had the effect of binding those businesses to the communities in which they were established. Previously, these businesses may not have felt any such ties, having forgotten perhaps that communities do not stop existing outside office hours. T-CAP also encouraged the adoption of school uniforms—a move that has

An Austin, Texas, a police officer distributes antidrug literature to city kids: crime prevention, if it is to be successful, involves work with the law-abiding as well as with criminals, with innocent children as well as with adolescent and adult offenders.

Children at Grimshaw Elementary School, Lafayette, New York, proudly show off their DARE diplomas after completing a course administered jointly by police and teachers. Experts agree that information and self-esteem are both key to an individual's ability to stand firm against the temptations offered by the drug culture.

proven time and again to encourage discipline and pride. It also promoted the idea of year-round schooling with several electives to discourage idleness and dropout.

Police have a part to play in education, too—both in the straightforward sense that they can act as "teachers," offering students the benefit of their experience, and in the sense that school visits provide an opportunity for the police to meet and form a relationship with younger people. Under T-CAP, existing **DARE** (Drug Abuse Resistance Education) programs were expanded.

ADOPT A COP

Police in Queensland, Australia, have an interesting way of getting their message into schools. Children "adopt" an officer from their local force for regular visits throughout their time at school. Talking with children on subjects from drug abuse to road safety, and from what to do when approached by strangers to the basics of home security, officers give these children vital tips on protecting themselves. Older students discuss issues such as actions and consequences and rights and responsibilities.

Chief Constable Norman Bettison
Card No 1

Perhaps as important as the content of these lessons, however, is the fact that children find themselves encountering a police officer in a caring, friendly role. This opens a line of communication between police and young people, and this, it is hoped, will endure into their teenage years and beyond.

Police in Liverpool, England, are trying to win hearts and minds by issuing their own set of "baseball cards" for local children to collect.

A tragedy in the making as boys play with a gun they have found in their father's bedroom: their new toy is, in reality, a lethal weapon. Every year across America, guns fired off by accident or in sudden anger end up destroying those families for whose protection they were originally bought.

YOUNG AND OLD

Education is for parents, too. T-CAP initiated programs to involve them more closely with the running of their children's schools and provided help with childcare to enable them to be more effective

Bike patrolmen in Montgomery County, North Carolina, take their work home with them in a novel way, going out for weekend rides with younger members of their communities. Informal contacts like this play a vital role in making the police force accessible.

parents. "Safe Houses" were opened to give children a safe place to play after school while parents were at work, and there were programs to train more qualified childcare providers.

For the elderly, special programs offered a range of trips and activities, which brought together young people and senior citizens. The young may often regard the elderly with a mixture of contempt and resentment; the old frequently view the young with cynicism and fear. Neither prejudice is fair, as many participants in T-CAP Fort Worth found, to their real pleasure. An "Adopt a Senior"

BUSY VACATIONS

"The Devil finds work for idle hands." Whoever originated that expression could easily have been thinking of the long summer vacation; trouble always seems to find some way of thriving in those endless, empty weeks. In France, local government offers young people in disadvantaged suburbs the opportunity to take part in all sorts of special programs: mainly sports and community activities, but also artistic and educational ones. The program started in 1981 in the city of Lyon in response to one particularly "long hot summer" in which serious violence flared up among gangs of idle teenagers. It proved such a success that the program was soon adopted throughout the whole of France—and not just during summer, but all significant school vacations.

A police officer puts in some hard labor with New York City students as they plant a garden together in Kirkville, New York.

program established special, and often mutually supportive, relationships between young people and elderly neighbors, to the advantage of both sides—and, indeed, the whole community.

A FORCE FOR CHANGE

Having encouraged so many citizens, local government, and businesses to change their attitudes and approaches, the Fort Worth Police Department could hardly exclude itself from the need to institute initiatives and reforms. In fact, change was little short of revolutionary. The police department serves an area that covers 300 square miles (777 sq km). This was divided into 12 NPDs (Neighborhood Policing Districts) in an effort to enable police work to return to its roots in the local communities. Seven of the new NPDs already have their own headquarters.

The headquarters for NPD 8, which opened November 2001, is a good example of the recent changes. Sited in a refurbished building 100 years old, it recognizably belongs to the community; indeed, community residents selected the location. The building will soon be available for use by citizens' advisory committees and similar groups; and residents will have the use of computers with Internet access. Impressive without being intimidating, the headquarters proclaims the commitment of police and people to one another—and the pride that both take in their neighborhood.

Left: Here, officers in riot gear stand by at a political demonstration in New York City. Sometimes, keeping the peace requires police officers to put on a show of almost military-style force.

SMALL-TOWN VALUES

When we think of an American small town, we think of a quiet and contented community free from crime. Here, everyone knows each other; here, there is true community spirit; here, you do not even need to think of locking your front door. That, at any rate, is the myth. Now, let us take a look at the reality.

It is true that such communities avoid some of the problems of big-city life. It is equally true, however, that it takes more than a white picket fence to keep out crime. There have always been vagrants and delinquents around who upset the peacefulness of small-town life. And in recent generations, the most far-flung country areas have been subject to many of the same social pressures as the big cities: family breakups, teenage drinking, drugs, and gangs.

The scale of the problem is often exaggerated—as it is in the urban centers—but there is no doubt that crime is now an everyday part of rural and small-town life in every part of the United States. Here, too, Americans have had to organize their own community-based crime prevention programs, also encouraged and led by local law enforcement agencies.

Left: A police officer helps a couple of school pupils cross the road safely. A police force concerned only with catching criminals is misunderstanding its function: the true police officer is the protector of his or her whole community.

Suburbs like this one outside Atlanta, Georgia, are often seen as epitomizing "the American Dream," and there is no doubt that thousands of city-dwellers yearn for such quiet and spaciousness. Yet the suburbs are by no means immune from the effects of crime: communities here have had to act together for their own protection.

FOR A CRIME-FREE FREEPORT

The smaller communities of America were once a byword for quiet coziness, but they are not feeling quite so comfortable now. With a population of some 24,000, Freeport, in northwestern Illinois, is the sort of small town in which generations of city-dwelling Americans have dreamt of living. Even here, however, people have recently felt the need to mount resistance against rising rates of crime. By 1994, there was a sense that youth crime was beginning to spiral. The wider community looked on, feeling powerless to intervene. Much of the reported crime was "minor"—vandalism and rowdiness, for example. Nonetheless, it contributed to a growing feeling of insecurity among the population at large and a steadily diminishing quality of life. In 1994, local police, politicians, officials, and residents came together to form the Freeport Coalition for a Safe Community, its mission, "to build a safe and healthy community for our children and families."

Fred Magine, Dave O'Connor, and Tom Cunningham work together at O'Connor's kitchen table to put together the newsletter of the Brittany Hills, Syracuse, New York, Neighborhood Watch. If crime has been a running sore on our society, the fight against it has drawn upon our deepest traditions of democracy and self-help.

A police officer hands out stickers and a key ring to a driver as part of a major public-relations "push" on seatbelt safety. Some sneer at such programs with all their accompanying paraphernalia of cartoon characters and other gimmickry, but the evidence suggests that they can help to fix important issues in the public mind.

At the center of the program is a drive to establish new Neighborhood Watch groups, bringing householders together with each other and with the police in the fight against crime. There have also been attempts to help those young people believed to be at risk of falling into crime. Freeport schools have placed extra emphasis on DARE, as city parks have established programs of activities for young people and their families.

Although the original impetus for the program came from concerned parents and adult householders, it was realized that young people could get tired of having grown-ups telling them what to do. One of the first actions of the Coalition, accordingly, was to set up a Youth Task Force, including 40 students representing grades 6–12. There has been help for adults, too, with the establishment of job-referral networks for the long-term unemployed. Programs have been introduced to provide parenting education so that Freeport's children can be given the best possible start.

In addition, the physical infrastructure of Freeport itself has been examined to see how it might usefully be changed, with surveys of street lighting and public spaces from a CPTED point of view.

THE VIRGINIA VERSION

Not all crime prevention programs need to be community-based (although all need the cooperation of the people among whom they are launched). Some may be initiatives of the local police.

In recent years, the Virginia State Police have been resourceful in tackling particular crime prevention problems in their own, largely rural, policing area. One of these, Rest Area Watch, was mounted in response to an escalating problem of crime at the state's roadside rest areas—a number of violent, in some cases homicidal, attacks were made at these isolated sites.

In a well-publicized campaign, patrolling officers made regular checks on rest areas. Critics said it was a lot of fuss and fanfare for what amounted to just a few minutes' policing time each day, but publicity is an important part of policing. If only one criminal sees

A BRAKE ON DRUNK DRIVING

For many years, drunk driving was not recognized as a crime. Since the offense is so often committed by members of the public who would never dream of breaking other laws, it has taken generations for police to instill the idea that it is indeed a crime—and a dangerous crime at that.

Increasingly, more and more young people are committing this crime. The 16–24 age group is responsible for an appalling 44 percent of America's alcohol-related nighttime fatal crashes, and for teenagers, drunk driving is the leading cause of death.

Students Against Driving Drunk (SADD)—the name was later modified to Students Against Destructive Decisions—was set up in Wayland, Massachusetts, in 1981. The aim was to unite students and their parents against a problem that was taking lives both young and old. At the center of SADD's philosophy is the Contract for Life, in which parents and students agree never to drive after drinking and to give each other rides when either is "above the limit."

Complete success can hardly be claimed—drunk driving remains a national tragedy—but drunk driving deaths among 15–19-year-olds fell 50 percent in 15 years.

the news on TV and decides it is no longer worth the risk, then crimes have been prevented and—very possibly—lives have been saved. Virginia's police officers are well satisfied with the program. Figures show a clear drop in this type of crime. Hence, the

A woman glows with the pleasure of having just been awarded a "good citizen's coupon" by a police officer under a program organized by Palo Alto, California, city police in partnership with local businesses. Coupons are handed out to considerate drivers, which can be exchanged for free goods, from cups of coffee to restaurant meals.

inauguration of similar programs: Convenience Store Watch and Worship Watch (based around local stores, churches, and other places of worship), in which special patrols have been established and advice on CPTED issues given.

COUNTRY CRIME

Many Americans, living in big cities, find it hard to believe there could be any such thing as rural crime: surely life is always

A Virginia State policeman carries out a search call in the course of a routine traffic stop: this is the everyday bread-and-butter of policing on our highways.

wonderfully quiet and peaceful in country areas? Rural dwellers know better: they may be spared the more spectacular gang-related violence of the more notorious inner-city areas, but in other respects they suffer much the same as their fellow citizens.

Vandalism, burglary, auto-related crime, drunk driving: such crimes have all helped blight the rural idyll in recent decades. In addition, farming folk must contend with problems their urban counterparts never dreamt of facing. Straight from the semimythical days of the Old West, for example, comes the all-too-real crime of cattle rustling—as grave a problem as it ever was in John Wayne's day, but not half so romantic.

Today's rustlers are more likely to drive 18-wheeler trucks than to ride ponies, and their motivation would have meant little to the more colorful outlaws of former times. Reporting on the problem for Statewide TV, Nebraska, Bill Kelly sums up the situation with depressing frankness: "No one really wants to admit just how easy it is to steal someone else's cattle. In a matter of minutes it can earn an enterprising thief more money than holding up a convenience store and with a lot less hassle."

Cowboys on a ranch in Texas select a calf for branding after the spring roundup: they would not be out of place in a Western movie. Other less-appealing traditions are also alive and well, unfortunately: cattle rustling today is a multimillion-dollar business.

Watchers of old-fashioned Western movies will be well aware of the time-honored tradition of "branding" cattle—of literally burning an owner's mark into the hide of a calf with a red-hot metal stamp. The brand stays with the animal as it grows: attempts to tamper with it are usually apparent, and it certainly cannot be removed, so the system allows the effective registration of America's entire livestock herd. Substantially the same method is used for branding as is to be seen in the old movies; now, however, it is backed up with a carefully-managed system of state- and nationwide record keeping, all strictly policed by a designated force of "Brand Inspectors."

In theory, then, the origins and ownership of any animal can be checked by a potential buyer as readily as those of any secondhand car; in practice, of course, things are not necessarily quite so straightforward. An unscrupulous rancher may well feel the risks of detection are worth running in light of the profits to be made from keeping stolen stock—while where as yet unbranded young calves are involved those risks become virtually nonexistent. Not surprisingly, there is a lucrative "black market" in unmarked animals like this, each of which may be worth $2,000 or more.

Right: Even well-intentioned trespassers can do enormous unwitting damage in rural areas: a "private property" notice explains the situation to the casual rambler. However, such a sign will do nothing to exclude the determined criminal, but it at least makes it clear that the land is looked after and kept under some sort of supervision.

RURAL CRIME UNIT

Since 1995, the sheriff's Office of Santa Clara County, California, has run its own designated Rural Crime Unit, geared toward the particular problems experienced by communities in agricultural areas. When the unit was founded, **trespassing** was a major problem, creating untold damage and disturbance each year, while theft was taking place on an enormous scale.

Cherries, strawberries, apricots, onions, and bell peppers were stolen by the truckload by determined and well-organized gangs. In its first year alone, the Santa Clara Rural Crime Unit recovered no less than 134,000 pounds (60,782 kg) of stolen garlic. Stock and equipment were also stolen, ranging from agricultural chemicals to irrigation pipe—in short, just about anything that was not nailed down. There were other problems, too, from dogs attacking livestock to remote farms and ranches used for drug labs by major traffickers. The financial costs aside, this crime wave was shattering the rural peace of mind.

The Rural Crime Unit has helped bring about a dramatic change, enabling rural homeowners, farmers, and ranchers to come together in their own defense. Offering everything from support in setting up neighbors' associations and crime watches, to the supplying of "No Trespassing" signs, they have made a great difference in a short time.

The city dweller's dream of the rural paradise is in stark contrast to the reality as it is experienced by South Carolina farming folk like these. For most country people, work is grueling and standards of living low. Such conditions could make some turn to crime.

HOME SAFE?

Crime prevention officers spend much of their time advising householders how to secure their homes against intruders. But when you have locked all the doors and windows, have you excluded all possible dangers? Sadly, in too many households, the answer is no. Domestic violence and child abuse can make a home a place of suffering.

Unfortunately, society is just now starting to comprehend the scale and seriousness of these crimes. Police forces are only now learning how to tackle such difficult offenses.

UNDER LOCK AND KEY

The most imaginative program in the world cannot substitute for basic precautions, and police forces throughout America spend much of their time advising householders on ways of making their homes and vehicles secure. **Double-mortise locks** to ensure firm front doors, peepholes and chains for checking callers, locks on windows, and timer-operated lights to make an empty house look occupied—there are lots of ways in which you can make a home a

Left: The "crack house" haunts the imagination as the home of all inner-city evil: this one was closed down and boarded up by police in Philadelphia. Yet many more respectable-looking houses in much more appealing locations than this may conceal appalling crimes and wretched sufferings of their own.

A friendly New York cop chats with two Dominican-American sisters on his beat: this sort of informal contact is the very essence of good community policing. Even so, the most insightful officer may miss the signs of domestic violence or other abuse.

less-inviting target for the criminal. Immobilizers, alarms, and tracking devices help safeguard a car. Crime prevention officers provide information and advice on all these measures.

BEHIND CLOSED DOORS

The home is not just a target of crime. In many cases, it is the source. Domestic violence and child abuse are a continuing problem in every part of the United States and in every social class. Partner violence has been described as a hidden crime. Not only is it

John Berry's witty photomontage illustrates the importance of keeping the home secure, but a padlock can make a prison as well as a place of safety. All too many in our society—especially women and children—find themselves trapped with abusers who make their lives an unrelenting round of fear and misery.

JAPAN'S GOOD RIDERS

Since 1996, more than one million motorcycles have been registered under Japan's innovative "Good Rider" program. Like all the best ideas (and certainly all the best crime prevention ideas), the initiative is quite simple. Anyone buying a motorcycle is encouraged to register it with the traffic authorities at the time of purchase. They are then given a sticker for the bike and a card to carry with them at all times. The vehicle's details are sent to the Japan Motorcycle Safety Association, which inputs all the information into a giant database that is accessible round-the-clock to any police officer in Japan.

This provides a means of restoring a motorcycle to its owner after it has been stolen, but the Good Rider program is also effective as a form of crime prevention. In particular, the program has drastically limited the possibilities of selling a stolen motorcycle to a dealer, a major disincentive for potential thieves.

characteristically committed in the privacy of the home, it is an area in which law enforcement has traditionally been reluctant to get involved. **Sexism** was a factor for a long time, of course. A predominately male police force was, at times, too quick to discount the claims of women victims, or was too willing to see men's version of events. Sometimes, women made accusations and then withdrew them, or refused to acknowledge when violence was only too clearly going on. Police were, therefore, wary of involving themselves in investigations that often proved a waste of everyone's time.

Today, we have a better understanding of the sort of situations in which domestic violence takes place, and the often-crushing pressures that prevent many victims from acting in their own defense. Fears of the violent partner conflict with fears of having to acknowledge the failure of the relationship and of the family breakup that will inevitably follow from invoking the law. There

The picture of suburban style and affluence—but as the sheriff's cruiser in the foreground indicates, this house in Cicero, New York, is also a crime scene. Domestic violence is often assumed to be confined to households at the very bottom of the social scale, but in fact occurs at every level of society.

Home security has to be seen in its totality, with crime prevention part of an overall strategy of safety—a strategy which even the youngest family members must understand, and in which all must feel involved. Here, a pair of Syracuse six-year-olds help a local fire officer with an evacuation plan for a typical family home.

may be complicating input, too, from in-laws and from friends—not to mention the attacker's insistence that, this time, he really will change. The recruitment of thousands of women to the police force has helped, as have the education of officers and the many campaigns promising victims support if they come forward.

SISTERS IN LAW

Like many other countries around the world, Brazil has had a long history of domestic violence and its police a shameful record of indifference toward a "private" matter. The reluctance of women to complain was reinforced by the contempt they received from the police if they tried to do so—which effectively gave the green light to continued violence.

Urged on by the State Council for the Status of Women, the authorities finally acted. The first of a series of all-women police stations was opened in Sao Paulo in 1985 to provide a reassuring environment for victims of violence. As well as offering sympathy, the women officers bring special experience to bear, as well as psychological help and—when needed—emergency shelter. Counseling is provided to male perpetrators of violence. Practice suggests that men find it easier to accept such help from women.

As with all crime prevention programs, one of its benefits is the signal it sends to the wider community. The opening of the women's police station—and of several others like it since—has made it clear that domestic violence is a serious issue. Indeed, there are encouraging signs that the new stations have had a major impact, both in cutting crime and in changing attitudes.

BREAKING THE CYCLE

The Elmira Police Department in New York State has, along with many others across America, a busy Victims' Services Unit. Its trained officers offer advice and support to those who have suffered all sorts of violent crime, but they have a special role in assisting those who have already been victims of domestic violence.

While no one would dispute that this sort of after-the-fact help is beneficial, can it really be described as crime prevention? Elmira officers are adamant that it can. Domestic violence, unfortunately, is seldom a one-time offense. Almost invariably, it is a long and ever-deepening cycle. In Britain, where four women a week are killed by their partners, a recent survey showed that victims had been beaten

A police officer in Philadelphia talks to men and women on his beat, building up a detailed picture of their lives and problems, and the current situation in the neighborhood. Community officers like this one have brought about a return to the first principles of policing, setting a premium on personal insight and local knowledge.

A New York City policewoman chats with a four-year-old girl— perhaps forming the basis for a relationship which will endure for many years. Experience has shown that dedicated community officers can become vital role models for young people who might otherwise be left adrift.

an average of 34 times before they finally reported their problems to the police. A timely intervention at an early stage can help prevent a whole succession of future crimes—including, perhaps, the crime of murder. Also in Elmira, there has been a determined drive by health care and social services to assist disadvantaged teenaged mothers with support during pregnancy and the early years of child rearing. Since 1978, visits by nurses have helped not only with health issues, but also with other aspects of parenting. This is clearly an admirable program, but, again, what does it have to do with crime prevention?

In fact, it has consistently been shown that neglected or abused children are more likely to turn to crime in later life. Elmira has done itself a favor by this act of community kindness. There has been a 66 percent drop in the arrest rate among those teenagers who passed through the program.

SUFFER THE LITTLE CHILDREN—AND THE ELDERLY, TOO

Children themselves are often victims of violence, of course—and even witnessing attacks on others can be profoundly traumatic: there is mounting evidence that such experiences can lead to the sort of psychological disturbance that tends to lead in its turn to violence and crime. Police in New Haven Connecticut have been working with psychologists at the city's Yale University in an interesting new program that attempts to address this problem. Basically, mental-health professionals and police officers have been comparing notes and sharing skills, enabling both to build a more psychologically sensitive approach to community policing together.

Attacks upon children by grown-ups not known to them are, in fact, comparatively rare, however large they may loom in the imaginations of anxious parents. But they can occur in reality, of course, and they are peculiarly distressing when they do, hence the need to instruct children in how they should respond to approaches from strangers. The message is simple enough, but it has to be driven home anew for every generation of children—who are naturally trusting. Be wary of attention from any adult not personally known to you—however nice or "cool" he may seem—and on no account get into a stranger's car. Registration programs

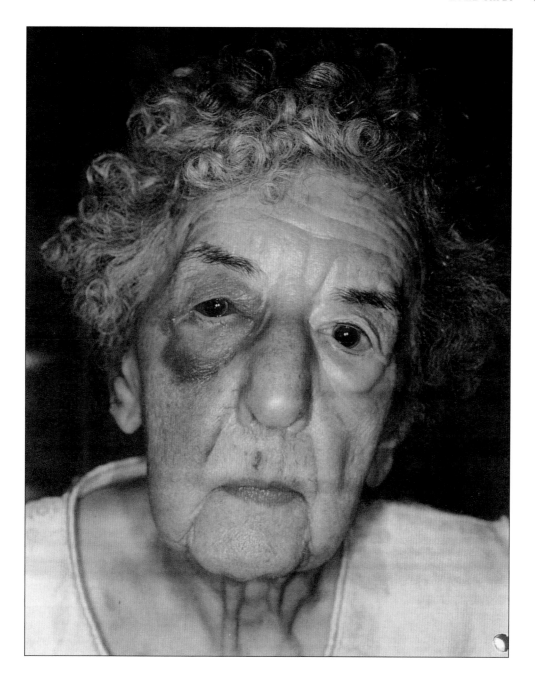

The face of trust betrayed: 87-year-old Rose Mackenzie had befriended the two teenage sisters who, in February 2000, would beat her savagely, steal her savings, and leave her for dead in her apartment block in London, England.

run by police and other law-enforcement departments have played an important role in keeping such offenses to a minimum, although they can always be evaded by a determined criminal. In response, some states and cities have passed laws demanding that parents be informed if any convicted child molester moves into their neighborhood, although this sort of program is controversial. Opponents point to the violation of the offender's civil rights, the difficulty he may have in reforming his life in an atmosphere of hate and suspicion—and, indeed, the risk that a "lynch mob" atmosphere may create greater dangers by driving convicted abusers completely underground. Advocates argue that the safety of children must override all other rights, and that more is to be gained than lost in openness on this issue. In addition to registering offenders, Albuquerque, New Mexico, registers children as well, so as to facilitate matters should the worst happen and they disappear.

Yet many experts in the field are concerned about the emphasis given to "stranger danger" given that an estimated 80 percent of child sex-abuse is committed by relations and aquaintances of the family. Public panic about the tiny number of media "monsters," they suggest, may be blinding us to the damage being done day in, day out to countless thousands of American children by apparently ordinary and decent parents, stepparents, babysitters, and family

Right: A policewoman radios in to headquarters: the active tracking of convicted child molesters by police remains controversial—while safeguarding the vulnerable in the short term, it risks driving offenders underground.

In New Haven, Connecticut, a police officer lifts up a little girl: some poor children have few positive experiences of adults in their lives. Studies conducted by the New Haven Police Department in conjunction with the city's Yale University have shown how the stresses of an unhappy home life may eventually find expression in criminal behavior.

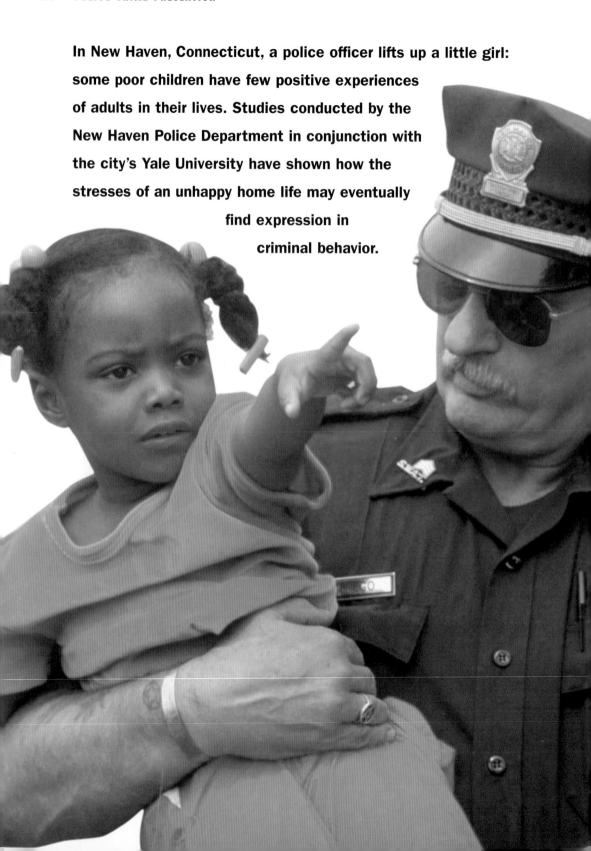

"friends." Such attacks may not involve headline-grabbing violence, but they create real terror and undermine self-esteem, and rob many victims of any hope of a happy grown-up life. Cynically exploiting as they do the child's natural instinct to trust and love, these abuses may well destroy emotional responses the growing individual will need if he or she is to form strong and enduring relationships in adulthood. Increasingly, we are waking up to the need to educate children out of an ignorance we once— quite mistakenly—prized as innocence, equipping them to recognize inappropriate behavior and to report any uneasiness they may feel to a parent or another caregiver. Listening is vital.

But children are not the only ones at risk: Burlington PD, California, is one of many America-wide making efforts to combat the growing (or perhaps only increasingly acknowledged) problem of "elder abuse." This term may cover anything from neglect on the part of relatives or caregivers to outright torture of the cruelest kind. Burlington officers are on the lookout for a range of warning signs, from physical bruising to psychological distress— or reluctance on the part of family or caregivers to allow the victim to be left alone with outside visitors. Listening is once again key: that old people may genuinely suffer from confusion has made it only too easy for their complaints of mistreatment to go unheeded.

GLOSSARY

Broken window theory: the sociological theory whereby evidence that a building or neighborhood is neglected "invites" further incidents of criminality

CPCA: the Crime Prevention Coalition of America was formed in the early 1990s to provide practical backup to local communities and organizations embarking on crime prevention programs

CPTED: Crime Prevention Through Environmental Design—the "planning in" of crime prevention measures to buildings and public areas, through thoughtful placing of street lamps, avoidance of concealed corners, and other such things

Criminologist: a person who studies crime, criminals, and punishment

DARE: Drug Abuse Resistance Education; a program involving police officers and educators aimed at teaching school students to say no to drugs and to maintain resolve in the face of what can sometimes be considerable social pressure

Double-mortise lock: a lock where the key turns twice, to secure a door or entrance for extra safety

Narcotrafficking: smuggling and trading illegal narcotics (drugs), such as cocaine

Neighborhood Watch: the oldest of the main community-based crime prevention programs, established by the National Sheriffs' Association in 1972; its aims are to encourage cooperation between ordinary citizens and law enforcement officers

Punitive: inflicting, involving, or aiming at punishment

Sexism: prejudice or discrimination based on sex, especially discrimination against women

Trespass: to wrongfully go onto another person's property

Truancy: the act of staying out of school without permission

Utopia: an imagined place of ideal perfection, especially in laws, government, and social conditions

Zero tolerance: a policing method inspired by the "broken window theory" in which small offenses, such as littering or drinking on the street, are vigorously pursued to maintain an overall sense that a neighborhood is cared for, and hence hostile to crime

CHRONOLOGY

1607: English colonists settle Jamestown, Virginia; volunteer militias are founded to defend the community against attacks by Native Americans and, later, the French.

1829: The world's first full-time professional police force, the Metropolitan Police, is set up to enforce law and order in London, England, on the orders of Home Secretary Sir Robert Peel.

1845: The New York Police Department becomes the first modern police force in the United States.

1860s: The first African-American officers serve in various police forces.

1910: Alice Stebbins Wells joins the Los Angeles Police Department as the nation's first female police officer.

1919: The Volstead Act imposes prohibition of alcohol, giving extra impetus to the already existing problem of organized crime; in response, police forces are compelled to become more professional, but also more remote from their communities.

1972: The first Neighborhood Watch programs are established on the initiative of the National Sheriffs' Association.

1977: The National Crime Prevention Council (NCPC) is established; it adopts McGruff the Crime Dog as its mascot for a high-profile campaign.

1980s: The work of George L. Kelling popularizes the broken window theory and introduces the idea of zero-tolerance policing.

1985: Teens, Crime, and the Community (TCC) is founded to coordinate crime prevention programs among America's young people.

1994: A new drive seeks to increase police presence at the community level under a major Community Oriented Policing Services (COPS) initiative.

2001: On September 11, terrorists attack the World Trade Center in New York City and the Pentagon in Washinton, D.C., by crashing aircraft into the buildings.

2002: The NCPC launches a "United for a Stronger America" campaign, aimed at bringing the energies, experience, and organizational skills of crime prevention groups (such as Neighborhood Watch) to help in the war against terrorism at a community level; a "Stop the Hate" campaign is launched to counter rising intolerance in the aftermath of the September 11, 2001, attacks.

FURTHER INFORMATION

USEFUL WEB SITES

For the National Crime Prevention Council (NCPC), see: www.ncpc.org

For the Crime Prevention Coalition of America, see: www.crimepreventcoalition.org

For teens, crime, and the community, see: www.nationaltcc.org

For the International Center for the Prevention of Crime, see: www.crime-prevention-intl.org

FURTHER READING

Kelling, George L., Catherine M. Coles, and James Q. Wilson. *Fixing Broken Windows: Restoring Order and Reducing Crime in Our Communities.* New York: Free Press, 1998.

Quarantiello, Laura E. *On Guard! How You Can Win the War Against the Bad Guys.* Lake Geneva, Wisconsin: Tiare, 1994. This book addresses the problem of crime prevention at household and neighborhood levels.

Sherman, Lawrence W. (ed). *Evidence-Based Crime Prevention.* New York: Routledge, 2002. This book provides a skeptical overview of current crime prevention policies.

ABOUT THE AUTHOR

Michael Kerrigan was born in Liverpool, England, and educated at St. Edward's College, from where he won an Open Scholarship to University College, Oxford. He lived for a time in the United States, spending time first at Princeton, followed by a period working in publishing in New York. Since then he has been a freelance writer and journalist, with commissions across a wide range of subjects, but with a special interest in social policy and defense issues. Within this field, he has written on every region of the world. His work has been published by a number of leading international educational publishers, including the BBC, Dorling Kindersley, Time-Life, and Reader's Digest Books. His work as a journalist includes regular contributions to the *Times Literary Supplement*, London, as well as a weekly column in the *Scotsman* newspaper, Edinburgh, where he now lives with his wife and their two small children.

INDEX

References in italics refer to
illustrations